COOKING THROUGHOUT AMERICAN HISTORY

What Was Cooking in Abigail Adams's White House?

Tanya Larkin

The Rosen Publishing Group's
PowerKids Press™
New York

The recipes in this cookbook are intended for a child to make together with an adult.

Many thanks to Ruth Rosen and her test kitchen.

Published in 2001 by The Rosen Publishing Group, Inc.
29 East 21st Street, New York, NY 10010

First Edition

Book Design: Danielle Primicer
Layout Design: Kim Sonsky

Photo Credits: p. 4 (John Adams) © Bettmann/Corbis, p. 4 (Abigail Adams) © SuperStock; pp. 7, 15 © CORBIS-BETTMANN; pp. 9, 11, 19, 21 by Thaddeus Harden; p. 12 © CORBIS; p. 16 © Bettmann/CORBIS.

Larkin, Tanya.
    What was cooking in Abigail Adam's White House? / Tanya Larkin.— 1st ed.
      p. cm.—(Cooking throughout American history)
    Includes index.
    Summary: Describes Abigail Adams, wife of the second president of the United States, her role as first lady, and some of the foods she served at various stages in her life.
    Includes recipes.
    ISBN 0-8239-5607-5
    1. Cookery, American—Juvenile literature. 2. Adams, Abigail, 1744–1818—Juvenile literature. [1.Adams, Abigail, 1744–1818. 2. First ladies. 3. Cookery, American.] I. Title. II. Series.

TX715 .L318 2000
973.4'4'092—dc21
[B]   00-028593

Manufactured in the United States of America

Contents

In the Footsteps of Martha and George

Abigail Adams was the wife of President John Adams, the second president of the United States. When George Washington was the first president of this country, John Adams was the vice president. John Adams was elected president and served for one **term,** from 1797 to 1801. The president's wife is known as the first lady. Abigail followed in the footsteps of Martha Washington, George Washington's wife. Abigail learned how to be a first lady by watching Martha Washington entertain guests. Some people felt that John Adams was a smart but grumpy president. Abigail made up for his grouchiness by being a warm and pleasant hostess to both government officials and everyday **citizens**.

◀ *These are pictures of John and Abigail Adams. Abigail was known as a warm and pleasant hostess.*

Equal Partners for Life

John Adams married Abigail Smith in 1764. They became the parents of five children. He and Abigail lived in Braintree, Massachusetts, not far from Boston. That part of their town later became known as Quincy. John Adams had been an important leader in the American Revolution. He helped to write the Constitution of the United States. Abigail and John wrote many letters to each other. These letters are important **documents**. They let us know about John and Abigail's marriage and about historical events. In one letter, Abigail asked her husband to consider the rights of women in the new Constitution. She was one of America's first **feminists**.

Abigail was also one of the best educated women in the colonies. John believed she was just as intelligent as he was. He called her his "partner for life."

This illustration shows the home where John and Abigail Adams lived in Quincy, Massachusetts. ▶

The New England Tradition

No matter where Abigail Adams lived, she never forgot her New England roots. Abigail always made sure that her kitchen **staff** prepared her favorite New England foods. These foods included white potatoes, cranberries, ham, and cider. Abigail liked cider better than the fancy drinks she served her important guests. John drank a large glass of cider every morning when he got out of bed. Abigail served traditional New England foods, like cream of corn soup and Indian pudding. The local Penobscot and Narraganset Indians had taught early settlers in New England how to cook meals with corn. The kitchen in the Adamses' cottage in Massachusetts had a large fireplace and brick oven. Abigail hung sage, lavender, and other herbs from the **rafters**. She even invented a cooler. She put slats in the kitchen floor to allow the cool cellar air to rise and keep food fresh. Refrigerators were not invented until much later.

Cream of Corn Soup

You will need:

¼ cup (59 ml) onion, finely chopped

3 teaspoons (15 ml) butter or magarine

3 tablespoons (44 ml) flour

4 cups (946 ml) milk

2 cups (473 ml) creamed corn

HOW TO DO IT:

☞ In a saucepan, combine onions and butter.

☞ Cook over low heat, for two minutes, until onions are soft.

☞ Add flour and stir until smooth.

☞ Slowly add milk and stir.

☞ Cook the mixture over low heat, for one minute, until thickened.

☞ Add creamed corn. Stir.

☞ Cook for five minutes, stirring often. Do not boil.

Serve in bowls. Serves six.

Corn was a food staple of the first settlers.
This dish was a favorite of President John Adams's.

European Elegance

The war for independence from England was fought from 1775 to 1783. During many of those years, Abigail and John lived in Europe so that John could serve the young nation as a **diplomat**. While in Paris, they often dined with Thomas Jefferson and Benjamin Franklin, who were also diplomats. Abigail soon developed a taste for elegant European style. When John Adams became president in 1797, the nation's capital was Philadelphia, Pennsylvania. Abigail knew how to save money on the president's salary of $25,000 and give successful parties at the same time. Independence Day had great meaning for the Adamses and for the other citizens of this newly founded nation. This day celebrated America's independence from England. On July 4, 1797, John and Abigail celebrated by serving their important guests cake, punch, wine, and a New England treat called Indian pudding.

Indian Pudding

You will need:

1 quart (946 ml) milk
½ cup (118 ml) cornmeal
2 tablespoons (30 ml)
   butter
½ cup (118 ml) dark
   molasses
1 teaspoon (5 ml) salt
1 teaspoon (5 ml)
   cinnamon
¼ teaspoon (1.2 ml)
   ground ginger
2 eggs

HOW TO DO IT:

☞ Have an adult preheat oven to 350° F (177° C).

☞ Pour milk in a heavy saucepan.

☞ Heat milk until bubbles appear at sides of pan.

☞ Have an adult help you add cornmeal to the top of a
   double boiler pan.

☞ Slowly add milk and stir.

☞ Cook for 20 minutes over hot water.

☞ In a small bowl, mix together butter, molasses, salt,
   cinnamon, ginger, and eggs.

☞ Slowly stir this mixture into the cornmeal mixture.

☞ Pour into a greased baking dish.

☞ Have an adult help you place the dish in a larger pan
   of hot water in the oven.

☞ Bake for one hour. Remove from oven.

☞ For a firmer pudding, cool for one hour.

Serve with ice cream or whipped cream. Serves 10.

GEORGE TOWN.

POTOWMAC RIVER.

EASTERN BRANCH.

Lat. Congreſs Houſe,
Long.

PART OF VIRGINIA WITHIN THE FEDERAL DISTRICT

PART OF MARYLAND WITHIN THE FEDERAL DISTRICT

...tory of the PLAN.

the Streets.

...NCES.

SCALE OF POLES.

Washington: The Third and Final Capital

In 1800, John Adams lost his second presidential election to Thomas Jefferson. That same year, the new town of Washington had become the third and final capital of the nation. Abigail Adams was not happy about packing up her family and belongings just to live in Washington for four months. That was when John Adams's term as president would end. On the way to meet her husband in the new capital, Abigail took a few wrong turns and got lost in the wilderness. When she finally arrived in Washington, she was shocked to find a treeless village set in the middle of a swamp. Only two government buildings were built. One was the Capitol building. The other was called the President's House. It stood on a freshly cleared dirt road called Pennsylvania Avenue.

◀ *This is the original map of the new capital city, which would become Washington, D.C.*

Moving Into the President's House

When John and Abigail moved into the White House, it was still called the President's House. Workers had been building it for eight years, but it was still unfinished. It took a lot of courage for Abigail and John to live in this unfinished house. The plaster on the walls was still damp. Abigail had her few **servants** set up open log fires in the rooms because there were no fireplaces yet. Unlike many rich families who lived in nearby Virginia, the Adamses had no **slaves**. Abigail felt that slavery was evil. After moving in, Abigail did much of the cooking and cleaning. She even did the family's laundry and hung it to dry in the large East Room. Abigail was impressed with the size of the the President's House. She called her new home a great castle, "built for the ages to come."

Abigail Adams liked to take a moment out of her busy day to enjoy the view from the ▶
mansion's windows of the Potomac River and the busy boat traffic.

The First Family in the White House

Abigail and John Adams made history by being the first presidential family to live in the official President's House. Just before Abigail arrived in Washington, John wrote a letter to her. In the letter he said that he prayed to heaven to bless the new house and everyone who would live in it in the future. "May none but honest and wise men ever rule under this roof," he wrote. One hundred and thirty years later, President Franklin Roosevelt had Adams's words carved on a **mantle** above a fireplace in the State Dining Room. Abigail and John's children were grown, but they raised their granddaughter Susan as their own child. Susan entertained her grandparents and kept them on their toes. Abigail often brought the child along as she did her housework.

◀ *Abigail and John Adams celebrated New Year's Day in 1801 with their family and important guests.*

Open to the Public

On New Year's Day in 1801, the President's House was opened to the public. The founding fathers of the United States thought that the President's House should belong to all of the people. American citizens of all different backgrounds were welcome to visit.

Abigail organized a fancy party for New Year's Day. She wore a velvet dress. She served cakes, tarts, creams, puddings, and other desserts to her guests. Abigail followed the **etiquette** she had learned during her travels in Europe. She greeted her guests from a chair that looked like a throne. John stood beside her and bowed to those who passed. He wore white powder in his hair and velvet **breeches** with silver buckles at the knees.

Flummery

4 cups (946 ml)
    blueberries
1 cup (237 ml) sugar
8-10 slices of bread, with
    trimmed crusts
butter
whipped cream
grated nutmeg

HOW TO DO IT:

☞ Have an adult help you preheat an oven to 350° F (177° C).

☞ Grease bottom and sides of baking dish.

☞ Wash blueberries and pour into saucepan.

☞ Add sugar and stir. Cook for 10 minutes.

☞ Spread butter thickly on one side of bread slices.

☞ Place bread, butter side up, in baking dish.

☞ Pour a little blueberry mixture over the bread.

☞ Repeat the last two steps, adding layers of buttered bread and blueberry mixture.

☞ Make sure the top layer is the berry mixture.

☞ Bake for 20 minutes. Chill until ready to serve.

☞ Serve with whipped cream topped with nutmeg.
Serves 6.

This New England dessert is sometimes made with raspberries or strawberries. Sometimes it is called "blueberry grunt."

19

A Busy Social Schedule

Abigail and John held the same weekly parties in the President's House as they had when they lived in Philadelphia. Like most important ladies, Abigail held afternoon parties for visitors every week. These receptions were called "drawing rooms" because they took place in the mansion's drawing room. When she wasn't entertaining at her home, Abigail visited at other people's homes. Both informal and formal gatherings took place at the President's House. Ordinary citizens **called on** the president, wandered around the house, and even peeked in the bedrooms. People wanted to find out what life was like for the president. Unlike today, there were very few guards surrounding the president. John and Abigail also held formal gatherings called **levees**. These gatherings were usually held in the Oval Room with its fashionable European chairs and sofas.

Raspberry (or Strawberry) Shrub

You will need:

½ cup (118 ml) lime juice
1 cup (237 ml) raspberry
    or strawberry syrup
3 cups (710 ml)
    ginger ale
2 cups (473 ml) apple
    cider (or apple juice)
orange slices

HOW TO DO IT:

☞ Pour all ingredients into a large punch bowl.
☞ Stir until blended together.
☞ Place orange slices on top of punch.
☞ Pour into punch cups.
Serves 10.

Shrub is an Arabic word meaning "drink."

Returning to Quincy

Abigail and John Adams looked forward to moving back to their hometown of Quincy, Massachusetts, when John's term was over. Back in Quincy, Abigail continued to receive guests, but more than anything, she loved to have all of her children and grandchildren at her dinner table. The Adamses had made their old farmhouse into a mansion fit for a president and his first lady. They called it Peacefield to remind them of the peaceful times they had enjoyed in the past. When their son, John Quincy Adams, became president of the United States, he made his father, John Adams, a proud man. John Adams died on July 4, 1826. That day was also the 50th anniversary of the signing of the Declaration of Independence. Abigail had died years earlier, in 1818. She was dearly missed by John, her "partner for life." In her lifetime, Abigail Adams was a true **patriot**, the wife of one president and the mother of another.

Glossary

breeches (BREE-chez) Short pants that fit tightly over the thighs and stop just below the knees.

called on (KAHLD ON) Made a visit.

citizens (SIH-tih-zenz) People who are born in or have the legal right to live in a certain country.

colonies (KAH-luh-neez) An area in a new country where a large group of people move, who are still ruled by the leaders and laws of their old country.

diplomat (DIP-lo-mat) Someone who conducts talks between nations.

documents (DOK-yoo-ments) Letters or other printed information that give proof of something.

etiquette (ET-ih-ket) A set of manners or customs required for social life.

feminists (FEH mih nists) People who believe in the social equality of men and women.

levees (lev-EES) Types of fancy afternoon parties held by an important person.

mantle (MAN-tul) A shelf above a fireplace.

patriot (PAY-tree-ot) A person who loves and defends his or her country.

rafters (RAF-ters) Beams below the ceiling that support the roof.

slaves (SLAYVS) People who are owned by other people and are forced to work for them.

servants (SUR-vants) People employed in a household.

staff (STAFF) A group of people who are paid to work for someone.

term (TURM) The limit of time one can be in office.

Index

Web Sites

To learn more about Abigail Adams, check out this Web site:
http://www.whitehouse.gov/WH/glimpse/html/ja2.html